Three Steps to Empower You in Any Situation

Inspired by Gerald Gould

Retold by B.B. Gould

And Presenting the Formula

CEO x 3R = PTSIT™

GG's Principle

Three Steps to Empower You in Any Situation

Published by:

Hawk & Hummingbird Press, Miami, FL

www.ggsprinciple.com

Cover Design and Layout by:

Launchpad Press, Cody, WY

www.launchpad-press.com

First Edition, July 2011

ISBN-13: 978-0-9834813-0-0

Contents

Acknowledgements

I would like to thank all of my guardian angels who watch over me and the "angels" on Earth—Doreen Curtis, Kim Martin, and the Rev. Dr. Marta Burke who pushed me forward. For Michelle Newman, who made it possible for me to devote so many hours away from my Boston terriers, Grace and Joy. For Heidi, in spirit, for the many years of love and devotion you gave to me after Gerry died, and to my spiritual mentors, Bishop J. Lloyd Knox and Dr. Barbara Simons, I would like to say a big thank you.

I would also like to thank Tom Bird for his enormous support in the birthing of this book. Your encouragement and technical advice was invaluable.

Introduction

Long before *The Secret* (Atria, 2006) exploded on the scene, ninety-eight words were given to Gerald Gould through divine inspiration. Gerald, or "GG" as he was known by his friends, was a successful business person, teacher, lecturer, mentor, and advocate for the power that comes through positive thinking and action. You may read his biography found later in this book. Called GG's Principle, these ninety-eight words condense all of the inspirational, self-help, self-empowerment books, CDs, and DVDs that have literally clogged book shelves in the last fifty years. What many have called "New Age" has been around since the times of Lao Tzu, Jesus, Buddha, and Mohammed.

Why do we look for outside help? Why don't we trust the power within? What happened in our history to make us want to seek assistance? Where is the first place we turn? Do we really need another guide? Do we really need one more set of directions?

I believe we do. Not because I want to sell books and devotional cards but because this message was given to my husband—a man who was so pure in thought, so loving and giving, that he received this message through divine inspiration. In our brief marriage of only one year, I was totally inspired when I first read his Principle. I told GG it needed to be shared with the whole world. Unfortunately, he was unable to share it before he passed over.

The Principle is divided into two parts. The first section presents three areas to which anyone can relate. Each day we all face challenges, have experiences and opportunities. These areas occur each day in some form; they are not unique to any one culture, any group of people, nor are they reserved only for adults. Children are also presented with these circumstances. The second part of the principle demonstrates what we do about these circumstances. Do we rise to the challenges, relish our experiences, and recognize opportunities? GG's Principle provides structure for the millions of people who seek self-empowerment and a way to achieve goals for personal growth.

I have included a list of quotations and affirmations. When used daily they create a positive environment. Famous persons are quoted throughout the book. An alphabetical list of these persons is provided after the Resources page (p. 50).

Also, please utilize the "Working with the Formula" section at the end of the book (pp. 54–56). You will find that it helps to list your challenges, experiences, opportunities, and those things that motivate and fulfill you.

Everyone thinks that his or her writing is unique, even if it is divinely inspired. In all of the self-help books I have read, none has offered such a succinct way of condensing the information as to be easily digested and implemented. GG's Principle does that. For adults, teenagers, and children alike, the formula *CEO x 3R = PTSIT* becomes a simple yet profound way of approaching all of the sum total of life's challenges and experiences, weighing the bad with the good. GG's Principle reminds us to stop and smell the roses while we relish all experiences and seize opportunities. Through discipline and determination, by taking the first step, we show the universe that we are serious about creating a reality that is harmonious to those around us and the things that make us tick.

Always a lifelong student of self-improvement and the power of positive thinking, GG was divinely inspired to write what he called GG's Principle. It has a potential for all humankind to be inspired. Only ninety-eight words in length, GG's Principle contains a powerful message with a formula that is easy to remember. It offers a concrete method of implementing the universal laws of attraction and fulfillment of dreams on a personal and practical level.

GG's Principle ©

CEO x 3R = PTSIT ™

I'm convinced there is an unbreakable golden thread that links every human being who has ever lived with those living today and those yet unborn.

With each new dawn all must face a share of new challenges, experiences, and opportunities.

I believe with discipline and determination anyone can learn to rise to each challenge; anyone can learn to relish the sum total of life's experiences, balancing the bad with the good, and anyone can learn to recognize opportunities that present themselves.

Only then do we become totally receptive to the God-given power to see it through.

AN UNBREAKABLE GOLDEN THREAD LINKS EVERY HUMAN BEING

East Meets West Meets East

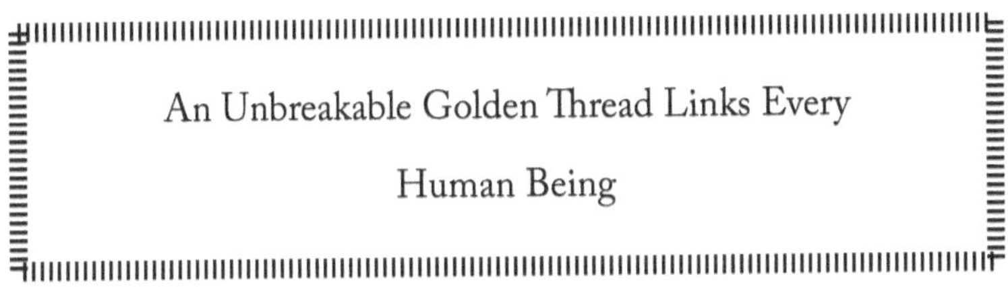

The Principle is already in the Universe. It has taken on many forms. Essentially, it is in the hearts and minds of all those seeking self-empowerment.

> "Every person, place, and thing on this planet is interconnected with love."
>
> —Louise Hay from *The Present Moment: 365 Daily Affirmations*

Beginning with the introduction of the Principle, GG believed we are all tied to each other with an invisible golden thread. Following in the traditions of Lynne McTaggart in her book, *The Field* (HarperCollins, 2002), the *Biology of Belief* (Hay House, 2008) by Bruce Lipton, the *Virus of the Mind* (Hay House, 1996) by Richard Brodie, and Amit Goswami's *The*

Quantum Activist (Blue Dot Productions, 2009), we find that our thoughts have connections.

Have you ever wondered how a Nobel Prize in chemistry can be shared by two independent laboratories on opposite sides of the planet? What are the mechanics of the same thought occurring almost simultaneously to two individuals who have never met? When the telephone rings, how do you know who is calling, even though you haven't seen or thought of that person in a very long time?

This golden thread is God's little spark of energy that resides in all of us from the Creator. The thread is in everyone we meet each day. Like it or not, we are all connected on this planet. We breathe the same air, see the same sun, look up at the same moon, and dream wonderful dreams for ourselves and our children.

EACH
NEW
DAWN
WE
ALL
FACE
NEW
CHALLENGES

PART I

Begin Each Day with a Smile and Get It Over With

Each New Dawn We All Face New Challenges

Everyday we meet new challenges. The kitchen sink may clog up just as you need to leave for a job interview. What do you do? Your computer may crash just as you were to participate in a seminar.

What challenges are you facing today?

The challenges we are facing in the world seem insurmountable. The jobless rate alone has created a feeding frenzy that is spiraling out of control. Persons who concentrate on the negative position of lack perpetuate the need to self-destruct. Prosperity and abundance elude them as they face daily challenges.

> "Focus your attention on the Now and tell me what problem you have at this moment."
>
> —Eckhart Tolle, *The Power of Now*

How do we face our challenges? Do we act on the impulses presented to us? As Wayne Dyer describes in his popular book, *Excuses Be Gone* (Hay House, 2009), it is not difficult to act on challenges. The many self-sabotaging behaviors can easily and quickly dissipate once we act on them.

What challenges are you facing right now? Imagine that they are gone. Picture yourself in the situation you desire.

EACH

NEW

DAWN

WE

ALL

FACE

NEW

EXPERIENCES

EXPERIENCED GOLF BALLS FOR SALE

Each New Dawn We All Face New Experiences

Along with the challenges we encounter each day, we face new experiences. GG teaches us to seek experiences that enlighten us.

Experiences are like challenges. Sometimes they crop up unexpectedly. Traveling down the road of life we might be presented with a new experience. We may become frightened and resist the experience. We may be reluctant to allow the experience to happen. What unexpected experiences have you encountered? We are given twenty-four hours each day. Within these hours, we can choose to allow the experiences to wither or to blossom. We should try to be open to new experiences and new ways of looking at them.

"God can dream a bigger dream for you than you can for yourself."
—Oprah Winfrey

EACH NEW DAWN WE ALL FACE NEW OPPORTUNITIES

WHEN YOUR SHIP COMES IN, DON'T BE AT THE AIRPORT

The third part of GG's Principle is opportunities. A cartoon character named Ziggy said once that when his ship comes in he will probably be at the airport. Many of us are waiting at the wrong place, at the wrong time, with the wrong people, with the wrong intentions. Many people do not realize that they can take control of their wellness. As a massage therapist I find that fact amazing. And, as a teacher in a massage school, I remind students that they are limited only by their imaginations. Upon graduation from massage school they will be competing with thousands of other therapists. In order to be successful, they must distinguish themselves, stand out, create a niche, and take the opportunities that abound to expand their businesses.

One way to have opportunities open up for you is to ask for help. Once that first step is taken, paths open that had previously been blocked. *The Secret* touched upon it, Louise Hay, in her book, *The Power is within You* (Hay House, 1991), expanded on it. It is a principle of the Universe. Until you make the first move and take the first step toward your goal, nothing happens. I can recount many incidences in my life that demonstrated this reality. The fact that this book has come into existence is one such reality.

Opportunities present themselves seemingly out of thin air. People are placed on your path to help you. You make connections that would not have been there before. Some people call these coincidences. I do not believe in coincidences. I believe in universal laws—laws that can be verified. Because of our free will, what we do with these laws is totally up to us. Our free will has been given to us so that we can be co-creators in our life experiences and opportunities. As co-creators in these experiences and opportunities, we have the ability to connect with them. We will see how this happens in the fourth part of GG's Principle.

> "God cannot fill that which is already full."
>
> —Mother Teresa (Blessed Teresa of Calcutta)

ANYONE
CAN
LEARN
TO
RISE
TO
EACH
CHALLENGE

Part II

'Rise and Shine and Give God the Glory, Glory'

Anyone Can Learn to Rise to Each Challenge

We must rise to challenges. When we write a thank-you note or e-mail, when we visit a neighbor in the hospital, we rise to the challenge. We rise to the challenge when we vote or take an unpopular stand against injustice. We rise to the challenge when we follow through on promises. We rise to the challenge when we are joined with others in a race against cancer. We rise to the challenge when presented with insurmountable obstacles and we find a solution.

"God is the source of my supply—Not my job, not my employer, not my spouse. My daily prayer:
God is the source of my supply. I do not become anxious or afraid. I stand firm and know the truth."

—Author Unknown

ANYONE CAN LEARN TO RELISH LIFE'S EXPERIENCES

Would You Like Relish on Your Hot Dog?

Anyone Can Learn to Relish Life's Experiences

After we rise to the challenge, GG advises us to relish the experiences. The word "relish" conjures up a different understanding. I do not relish *relish* on my hot dogs, but I certainly relish life. What does it mean to relish life? To relish life, one must reach for the gusto. Life is a bowl of cherries to be enjoyed. To relish life means to be deeply immersed in it, savoring all of it, while at the same time balancing the bad with the good.

Growth comes from each experience. We can either learn from our experiences or repeat them. I like to use the popular phrase, "if you keep doing the same thing, you will get the same results." Veiled in GG's Principle is the driving force of divine love. When we truly have love for ourselves and others, nothing is impossible. The divine power that propels us forward is the same power to get us through any situation. "With God all things are possible" is not a pie-in-the-sky affirmation to be taken lightly. It has been proven time and time again. Another favorite saying I learned from my mother, "God won't put anything on your shoulders that you, with God's help, can't handle." The same God who leads you to it can lead you through it.

ANYONE CAN LEARN TO RECOGNIZE OPPORTUNITIES

Anyone Can Learn to Recognize Opportunities

So how do you recognize opportunities? Sometimes opportunity knocks. A popular television commercial features a likeable car salesman banging on the television screen as he says, "I'm Mr. Opportunity, and I'm knocking." Well, I'm not so sure all opportunity knocks. It hits you in the head sometimes. Unfortunately, we become so preoccupied with the pain in the head that we fail to see the answer to a problem that presented itself.

We must be in the flow, the "Zone," the receptive state to recognize opportunities.

How do you get in that state? It only takes a few steps. First, you must be willing to see the glass "half full" rather than "half empty." There is power and possibility in positive thinking. By making a conscious effort to think positively you can be receptive to change. If you keep doing what you have been doing, you should keep on getting the same results. "Be the change you want to see." How does this happen? Let's take a look at what our Creator promises.

> "Procrastination is the grave in which opportunity is buried."
>
> —Author Unknown

BECOME
TOTALLY
RECEPTIVE
TO THE
GOD-GIVEN
POWER
TO
SEE
IT
THROUGH
(PTSIT)

We Have Power Surges

Become Totally Receptive to the God-Given Power to See It Through

By rising to the challenge, relishing life's experiences, and recognizing opportunities that come your way, you will be given the power to see it through.

GG's Principle is a simple, practical way of living life to the fullest.

As you generate energy toward your goal, the power rises up to meet the power from the Universe coming down toward you. This higher power will always be there. This higher power will help open up avenues of opportunities. This power given to you will help you to rise to any challenge and overcome it.

> "Therefore I tell you, whatever you ask for in prayer, believe that you have received it, and it will be yours."
> Mark 11:24 (*NIV)*

Barriers that had previously stopped you from becoming the person you desired to be are removed. Doors, previously closed, are opened. A renewed strength consumes you. You have risen to the challenge, relished the experiences, and recognized the opportunities, and you now have the power to see it through.

> "Anything you can do or dream you can, begin it. Boldness has genius, power, and magic in it."
> —Goethe

Now let's look at two words found within GG's Principle: "discipline" and "determination." Christians have studied the lives of the Disciples. Leonardo da Vinci painted his famous "Last Supper" featuring Jesus with the Disciples. What exactly does it mean to be a disciple or to apply discipline to your life? You must decide to follow a set of standards, rules, and a way of life. There is a popular Bible translation entitled *The Way* (Tyndale House, 1973), Lao Tzu spoke of following the *Tao Te Ching*. Muslims have the Five Pillars of Islam to follow.

Where does this discipline come from? It begins with a decision. When you see yourself drug-free, or see yourself having health and abundance, abundance flows. It is as if all gates were opened.

This is the determination to be in that Zone—in that image you have of yourself. I believe determination is a byproduct of an inward shift. This mind shift occurs once the decision to change occurs. Nothing happens until that inward shift occurs.

Jesus said, "I came so that you could have life and have it abundantly."
John 10:10 (*NIV*)

This way of living is not new, not New Age, not even exclusively Christian. It is a universal law that is available to all. In the Bible it is written that all we have to do is ask and it will be given to us. According to the brilliant writings of Louise Hay, you can have what you ask for because you have made the decision—you have the determination and the discipline to see it through. In whatever form you believe the universal power to be—by whatever name you call it—energy has been set in motion to bring forth a manifestation of that which is acted upon.

Where does one begin? When W. Clement Stone was a young boy, he sold newspapers to customers in a coffee shop while they ate their breakfast. He could have stood out in the cold Chicago winters, but he seized an opportunity to capitalize on the captive diners. Stone went on to create one of the most successful insurance companies in America.

> "Anything you can conceive and ardently believe, you can achieve."
> – W. Clement Stone

Everything begins as a mental equivalent. Great cathedrals first appeared in the minds of the architect and builder. A building isn't built by looking at one brick at a time: it is built with the finished product in mind.

For self-empowerment, begin with the end in mind. See yourself happy, healthy, and whole. You may not reach your goal if you worry about how you are going to achieve your new Self. You are given introductions to people who can help you when you realize that we are all connected. Networks create opportunities for you to move toward your goal.

When you take the first step toward your goal, you may realize that you need to move in another direction. If you don't move in the new direction or stay in one spot, you certainly will not be moving toward your goal. The key to any self-help or self-improvement program is to take the first step. In other words, implement what the program is suggesting. You have to begin to do what the program suggests.

Applying the Formula

CEO x 3R = PTSIT™

C – Challenges

E – Experiences

O – Opportunities

R – Rise to challenges

R – Relish experiences

R – Recognize opportunities

P – Power

T – To

S – See

I – It

T – Through

Five other buzz words we can use in addition to the ninety-eight words that make up GG's Principle are *motivate, encourage, discover, enable,* and *fulfillment.* What motivates you? Have you ever taken on a project only to find yourself at the end of the day completely re-energized? And did you find that you accomplished even more than you set out to accomplish? Isn't it funny how that works?

When a friend is down, sometimes a word of encouragement from you is all it takes to bring him or her out of a "blue period." We all have persons in our lives who brighten our day by giving us an encouraging word, a pat on the back, a phone call, or an e-mail. I would encourage you to be an encourager.

Remember when you were a child and you made a new discovery? Perhaps you discovered a butterfly emerging from its cocoon. On her CD, *Follow Your North Star* (Sounds True, 2005), Dr. Martha Beck describes the metamorphosis of the butterfly in thrilling detail. She goes on to describe how your new image can emerge. You can make a discovery each new day. The discovery may be the challenges you face. The discovery may be that a new experience is wonderful. Or you may receive an answer to a problem—thus enabling you to move toward a long-awaited goal. What other things enable you?

However it is that your dreams are fulfilled, know that "the universe is unfolding as it should," as written in 1927 by Max Ehrmann in his poem called "Desiderata." What will it take to fulfill your dreams? Have you lost your dream? Go back to the beginning of your journey. Ask the Universe what it is that truly motivates you. What would you do if you knew you couldn't fail?

Are you ready to receive this power? Are you ready to have an abundant life? Are you ready to accept a higher Self—a Self driven by universal law? Put GG's Principle into practice. Embrace all of the separate parts. Know that this principle has been shared with all humankind.

DAILY BREAD

Use these on a daily basis to help you
Rise to **C**hallenges, **R**elish **E**xperiences, and
Recognize **O**pportunities

Day 1
When life gives you lemons, make lemonade.

Day 2
When life gives you lemons, give them away and get something you want.

Day 3
If you keep doing the same thing, how can you expect different results?

Day 4
"Be the change you want to see." —Gandhi

Day 5
"Whether you think you can or you think you can't – you are right." —Henry Ford

Day 6
"If life is just a bowl of cherries, what am I doing in the pits?" —Erma Bombeck

Day 7
"A ship in harbor is safe, but that is not what ships are built for." —John A. Shedd

Day 8
To move in the direction of your dreams you have to work the oars.

Day 9
"Ask and it will be given to you." —Jesus Matt 7:7 (NIV)

Day 10
"Seek and you will find." —Jesus Matt 7:7 (NIV)

Day 11
"Knock and the door will be opened for you." —Jesus Matt 7:7 (NIV)

Day 12
"The Lord is my shepherd; I shall not want." —King David Psalm 23:1 (KJV)

Day 13
"I can do all things through Christ who strengthens me." —St. Paul Phil. 4:13 (NIV)

Day 14
"Nothing can separate us from the love of God." —St. Paul Romans 8:39 (NIV)

Day 15
"In the beginning was the word." —John 1:1 (KJV)

Day 16
"You are a child of the universe, no less than the trees and the stars." —Max Ehrmann

Day 17
"It takes guts to leave the ruts." —Robert H. Schuller

Day 18
"Tough times never last but tough people do."
—Robert H. Schuller

Day 19
"A journey of a thousand miles begins with one step."
—Lao Tzu

Day 20
"All you need is love." —The Beatles

Day 21
You are loved.

Day 22
They can fly because they think they can.

Day 23
"Hold fast to dreams; for if dreams die, life is a broken-winged bird that cannot fly." —Langston Hughes

Day 24
"What would you dream if you knew you couldn't fail?"
—Robert H. Schuller

Day 25
"Work as if everything depended on you, and pray as if everything depended on God." —St. Augustine

Day 26
Dream so big that only you and God can accomplish it.

Day 27
"Do not do to others that which you wouldn't want others to do you." —Maimonides

Day 28
Do not pray for an easy life. Pray to be strong for whatever life has to offer.

Day 29
"Just do it." —Nike

Day 30
Believe.

Day 31
The glass is half full.

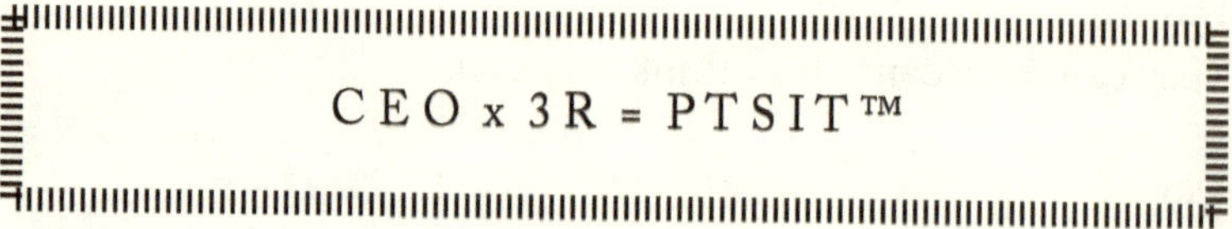

Daily Bread to Use with Children

Day 1
"Jesus loves me, this I know." —Anna Warner, David McGuire, and William Bradbury

Day 2
"Jesus loves the little children; all the children of the world, red and yellow, black and white." —Herbert Woolston and George Root

Day 3
"Do unto others as you would have them do unto you." —The Golden Rule

Day 4
"All creatures, great and small…the Lord made them all." —Cecil Alexander and Martin Shaw

Day 5
"Now I lay me down to sleep. I pray the Lord, my soul to keep."

Day 6
"Little David was small, but oh my…" —George Gershwin

Day 7
"Let there be peace on Earth, and let it begin with me." —Seymour Miller and Jill Jackson

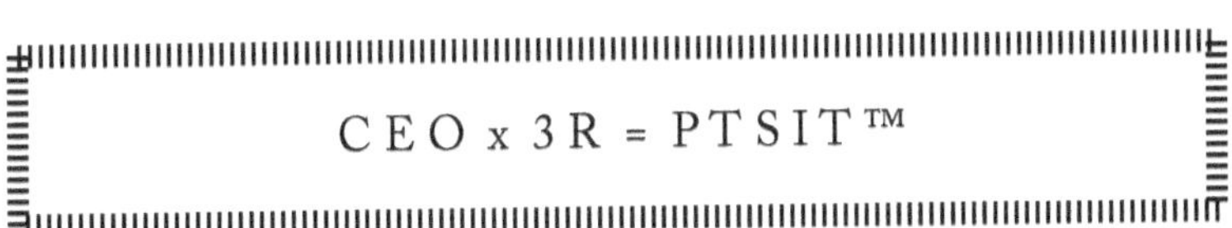

Remember Your ABCs

A — Avoid negative people, places, and things.

B — Believe in yourself.

C — Consider things from all possibilities.

D — Don't give up, and don't give in.

E — Enjoy life now; yesterday is gone.

F — Friends are given treasures.

G — Give more than you planned to give.

H — Hang on to your dreams.

I — Ignore those who try to discourage you.

J — Journal your results.

K — Keep on trying; it gets easier.

L — Love yourself first and most of all.

M — Make it happen.

N — Never think negatively.

O — Open doors that have been closed.

P — Practice brings results.

Q — Quitters never win; winners never quit.

R — Remember the Golden Rule, "Do Unto Others."

S — Stop procrastinating.

T — Take control of your own life.

U — Understand yourself; you'll understand others.

V —Visualize your needs.

W — Want peace and harmony in body and soul.

X — "Xcellerate" your efforts to improve.

Y — You are unique; you are special.

Z — Zero in on your target. Go for it! Live!

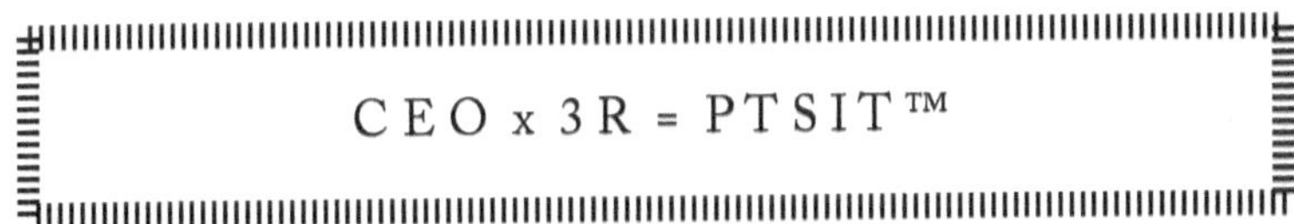

GG's Biography

Born in Queens, New York, Gerry Gould (GG) was a studious young man. He would rather listen to the weekly radio broadcast of the preacher/ theologian Harry Emerson Fosdick than eat. Gerry's mother would have to call him away when supper was ready. Gerry devoured every book that Fosdick wrote, and he adopted him as his mentor. "HEF" was the way Gerry referred to him. It was this early introduction to positive thinking that inspired GG to become a leading proponent of taking the bull by the horns and riding it. Gerry was always a person who followed his heart and stepped out on faith.

While Gerry was in graduate school, he visited his beloved maternal grandmother, Adele, and her husband who had a debt collection agency in Miami. Gerry returned to Queens and told his professor and advisor that he was moving to Miami, much to their chagrin. His grandmother sold the Royal Collection Agency to Gerry soon afterward. Determined to succeed, Gerry went feet-first into business with his sink-or-swim attitude. This was one of the major challenges Gerry met in his life—a challenge to which he would rise.

Many years later, Gerry would become a teacher and mentor to collection agents all over the United States. He was on the committee to draft the Fair Debt Collection Laws, which are still in effect today. To read more about this fascinating part of Gerry's life, I encourage you to read his book, *And Forgive Us Our Debts* (Gould, 1989). It is a hilarious history of the debt collection industry.

Always a life-long student of self-improvement and the power of positive thinking, Gerry was divinely inspired to write what he called GG's Principle.

I met GG when I was giving a monologue one Sunday morning in our Methodist church in Miami. Later, he approached me and said, "We have something in common. I'm GG and you're B. B." Of course, I was not immediately impressed, figuring it was some "line" that he was using. Our circle of friends kept bringing us together and we discovered that we had a lot of similar experiences and interests. One such interest was to succeed in business.

Later, we were married and spent only one glorious year together. We did more in one year than many couples accomplish in a lifetime. We travelled to Alaska, my niece's wedding in St. Maarten, and we opened a chair massage business in a local mall. Each month we would surprise each other by celebrating the twenty-first day of the month—our anniversary date.

While preparing for our first anniversary trip, Gerry suffered a fatal heart attack. This came as a complete shock; he had just passed his yearly physical with flying colors.

*****

Let's go back a few months into our marriage. I had just begun a business as mentioned above. I had partnered with another massage therapist who really knew the business, having successfully operated several chair massage businesses around the state. My business partner decided to relinquish his half in the business, leaving it all to me. There I was, a newlywed having to sink or swim with a new business, just like Gerry at the beginning of his collection agency.

Gerry was a godsend. Since he had successfully run his business for many years, he knew marketing strategies, and, of course, he was a real people person. Gerry told me that he would not let me fail. Our business blossomed.

Unfortunately, Gerry died after one year. Because our business in the mall took so much of our time, Gerry never got around to sending GG's Principle to be published. Even though I felt Gerry's spirit at the mall, I needed to move on. Now I have written this book based on his original ninety-eight words.

*****

Many people ask me why I chose the hawk and feathers for the logo of GG's Principle. Gerry and I were proud of our Native American roots, small though they were. Shortly after his death, a hawk appeared seemingly out of nowhere. Living in the city, it was unusual to see a hawk. My neighbors saw it as well. It would come to my yard and then fly off, disappearing from view. As described in the book, *Animal Speak* (Llewellyn, 1993), there is a belief among Native Americans that certain animals appear to us during our daily lives to guide us or to teach us a lesson. I definitely felt nurtured whenever I saw "Gerry's Hawk."

The first time I read GG's Principle I immediately saw the potential for all humankind in its ninety-eight words of self-empowerment. With the application of the formula, I knew it could easily be implemented by people worldwide. I told Gerry that his principle was huge and that it needed to be shared with the world.

I asked him how he came up with it. He told me that God gave it to him through the voice inside him. It was at that moment I knew this divinely inspired writing had to be published.

Well, now is the time. In fact, *The Law of Attraction*, *The Secret*, and the latest works of Louise Hay and Wayne Dyer have all paved the way with their hard work so that the Universe is ready to open up for GG's Principle.

B. B.'s Biography

B. B. Gould is a self-described "lifelong Methodist." An angel visited her when she was six years of age. She has always believed in guardian angels. Was this the voice of God, a guardian angel, the Holy Spirit, or a higher self? Her mother told her, "Always listen to that voice." That voice has spoken to her on numerous occasions.

She considers herself to have had an extremely fortunate childhood; she felt loved. Everyone around her was happy and she remembers hearing laughter long into the night in Cincinnati, where she was born, and Miami, where she was raised. When she was thirteen a minister in her church told her that she wasn't like the other members of the Methodist Youth Fellowship. She seemed more mature, the pastor said, self-actualized. She took this in and developed an individual self that seemed to separate her from others. She began studying church history and participated in district events. She was on her way to becoming a certified lay speaker.

After graduating from the University of South Florida, she began teaching biology in Miami. Five years later she attended Emory University and earned a graduate degree to become a school library media specialist. Even though she had very little money, she knew that she could go anyway. This is an interesting story in her life. It exhibits manifestation of money and the pursuit of a dream.

During her thirtieth year with the school system, another path opened up for her: she pursued a lifelong interest in massage therapy. Retiring from education in June 2001, she achieved her goal of national certification in massage therapy. She has since taken advanced studies in the Usui method of Reiki energy healing, something that she incorporates into her massage practice.

Returning to her first love of teaching, she is now holding classes in massage therapy.

Her hobbies include gardening, singing, golfing, and public speaking. She shares a tropical home in Miami with her two Boston terriers, Grace and Joy, and a big yellow cat named Benji.

She firmly believes that the power to change the world lies in each of us. She is fond of quoting Margaret Mead, who once said, "Don't underestimate the power of an individual to make a difference in the world. It is the only thing that has."

Closing Remarks

I gave birth to this book for me, for GG, but mostly for you: the reader. How you approach this gift is up to you. I wish I could say, "I guarantee that it will change your life." I do know that you won't be the same if you apply the two parts of the Principle. Take the formula, *CEO x 3R = PTSIT*, and dissect it, memorize it, and apply it. Keep a journal to record your challenges, experiences, and opportunities. Record "aha" moments, or as I prefer to call them, God moments. Write how you have risen to your challenges, relished your experiences, and how you have recognized and acted upon opportunities.

Please visit the website, *www.ggsprinciple.com,* and e-mail me. I hope to compile another book that will include the stories of reader journeys toward utilizing GG's Principle. I anxiously look forward to your results.

REMEMBER THREE STEPS TO EMPOWER YOU IN ANY SITUATION

STEP 1
RISE TO CHALLENGES

STEP 2
RELISH EXPERIENCES

STEP 3
RECOGNIZE OPPORTUNITIES

HOW I USED THE THREE STEPS OF GG'S PRINCIPLE

Oil Change – Guardian Angel

For several days I kept getting the impression to check my oil, to get an oil change—something to do with the oil in my car. I even looked in my driveway to see if there was an oil leak. Finding nothing, I went on my way.

One day I noticed my neighbor was checking his oil and I asked if he could help me check mine. Now, I know how to pull the dipstick, but something told me to ask for help. To my astonishment we discovered that there was no oil on the dipstick—not even a smudge. I had taken a 200-mile road trip the previous day. I realize I could have caused severe engine damage. My neighbor was an angel. He went to the store and purchased two quarts of oil for my car and poured it in immediately.

Sometimes our guardian angels give us little nudges; sometimes the message is less subtle. How we rise to the challenge or recognize these opportunities determines how we approach life.

Loan Modification

In 2009 I received a notice from my mortgage company that my monthly premium was increasing from $1,800 to $2,300 a month starting in January 2010. The timing couldn't have been worse. It seemed that the bottom was dropping out of everything and almost everyone I knew was experiencing similar skyrocketing changes in their financial obligations.

Let me set the scene. In August 2004 I established a chair massage business in a local area mall. GG and I had married that same month. The business demanded long hours and was very expensive to operate. Each month brought a rent and liability insurance of $5,000. I could see that the business was going to take a lot of hard work to make it successful. I had just signed my second-year lease when GG died unexpectedly from a heart attack. There I was, a new widow without the major support of my partner. The mall would not release me from my contract. For the entire year I dipped into my savings and incurred considerable credit card debt. When the year ended I was facing over $100,000 in debt. My pension and massage income could cover my living expenses so long as the monthly payments stayed about the same.

Fast forward three years. The banks wanted a lot more money each month. I realized I was in real financial trouble. The old expression "robbing Peter to pay Paul" took on an intimate meaning to me. There were some months when I had to make a decision on which bills I would pay. To show how naïve I was, I worried that my car would be repossessed when I was late with payments. I even thought about parking my car away from my house so that it wouldn't be here when the repo man came to tow it away. Living in fear of collections is a terrible way to live. To save money each month I whittled away at my services—cutting back on telephone features such as caller ID—stopped eating out, and other luxuries I had taken for granted.

At the time I did not realize how I was attracting gloom and doom. I had forgotten about using positive affirmations, visualizing the desired outcome and fervently believing in their realizations.

Because money was so tight I rarely ate out. However, one day I stopped for lunch and observed a flier advertising an attorney who presented loan modification seminars. Here was an opportunity presenting itself to me. I took a chance. Or, more precisely, I *stepped out in faith.* Qualifying for a loan modification was a tedious process, but I believed with all my heart that I was supposed to stay in my home. I didn't know how, but I knew I was going to receive a loan at a lower rate with a lower monthly premium. The process to achieve my dream took fourteen months.

I keep coming back to different scenarios and challenges occurring throughout my life. There is one thread that connects these situations. One thing is certain. I became empowered after I applied GG's Principle to the situation.

Relish

People are constantly asking me how I can be so cheerful, especially during the challenging financial times I have just experienced. Well, let me describe it this way. There exists a place within each of us that seems to be a calming presence; a godliness that I have recognized as being spirit-filled.

Please don't misunderstand me. I am not a saint by any stretch of imagination. On the contrary, I struggle with emotions and personality quirks like everyone else. The big difference I have seen comes from the analyzing of this inner glow, this feeling of contentment. Whether it is a sense of purpose, knowledge of belonging to a power greater than me, an inner compass is there to guide. The power to see it through is generated from this inner place, a place that is the golden thread connecting me to the cosmos.

Through the ages many philosophers have described this. The quantum physicists are using their scientific formulations and explanations to say that God exists in each of us, and that we are all connected.

Take a step in the direction of your opportunities. Look around; they do exist. After taking the first step, you will be amazed at the new opportunities opening up to you.

I remember wondering how I was going to be able to publish this book. I prayed for guidance. I had written the book but let it sit for months with little input. One day I received an e-mail describing a program that basically said I didn't need to know all the steps to get to the end of my goal: I just needed to take the first step that was laid out to me. I also believed in the end result. Martin Luther King Jr. said it this way: "You don't have to see the entire staircase in order to get to the top."

Power to See It Through (PTSIT)

I encourage you to use the "Working with the Formula" section in the back of this book. By the simple act of writing your responses, you will feel a movement toward your goal. Blockages will be removed. And, if you do not have a goal, the exercise can assist you in clarifying one.

By recalling memorable experiences you recreate the physical environment and sensations you felt when those experiences first occurred. The more positive the experiences, the stronger the sensations will be. These sensations can be summoned again and again. The frequency of a sensation creates strong bonds along the neural pathways. These bonds reinforce desired outcomes. What you put your attention on becomes your intention; this becomes your reality. Getting back to the "glass is half full" description creates a positive perception. A cascading effect occurs, producing more neural pathways in which you establish stronger bonds toward your desired goal. This is the law of attraction in the Universe.

RESOURCES

Andrews, T. (1993). *Animal-Speak: the Spiritual & Magical Powers of Creatures Great & Small*. St. Paul, MN: Llewellyn.

Beck, M. (2005). *Follow Your North Star*. CD. Boulder, CO: Sounds True.

Brodie, R. (1996). *Virus of the Mind: the New Science of the Meme*. Carlsbad, CA: Hay House.

Byrne, R. (2006). *The Secret*. New York: Atria Books.

Dyer, W. (2009). *Excuses Begone! : How to Change Lifelong, Self-defeating Thinking Habits*. Carlsbad, CA: Hay House.

Goswami, A. (2009). *The Quantum Activist*. DVD. Blue Dot Productions.

Hay, L. (1991). *The Power is Within You*. Carlsbad, CA: Hay House.

Hay, L. (2007). *The Present Moment: 365 Affirmations*. Carlsbad, CA: Hay House.

Lipton, B. (2008). *The Biology of Belief: Unleashing the Power of Consciousness, Matter & Miracles.* Carlsbad, CA: Hay House.

McTaggart, L. (2002). *The Field: the Quest for the Secret Force of the Universe.* New York: HarperCollins.

Schuller, R. H. (1985). *The Be (Happy) Attitudes: Eight Positive Attitudes That Can Transform Your Life!* Waco, TX: Word Books.

Schuller, R. H. (1983). *Tough-minded Faith for Tender-hearted People.* Nashville: Thomas Nelson.

Schuller, R. H. (1984). *Tough Times Never Last, but Tough People Do!* New York: Bantam Books.

Tolle, E. (1999). *The Power of Now.* Novarto, CA: New World Library.

PERSONS MENTIONED IN THE BOOK

Martha Beck — Author & life coach

Erma Bombeck — Author & humorist

Richard Brodie — Author & speaker on memetics

Buddha (Siddhartha Gautama) — Spiritual teacher, founder of Buddhism

Rhonda Byrne — Television writer & producer

Wayne Dyer — Author & motivational speaker

Max Ehrmann — Attorney & author

Henry Ford — Industrialist

Harry Emerson Fosdick — Author & theologian

Mahatma Gandhi — Political leader through non-violence; father of India

Amit Goswami — Quantum physicist, author, inspirational speaker

Louise Hay — Author & motivational speaker

Langston Hughes — Novelist, playwright & poet

Jesus — Messiah, teacher, prince of peace

King David — Poet, musician & king

Lao Tzu — Philosopher & founder of Taoism

Bruce Lipton — Cell biologist, author on epigenetics, speaker bridging science & spirit

Maimonides — Medieval Jewish philosopher

Lynne McTaggart — Author, journalist & speaker on the science of intention

Margaret Mead — Anthropologist

Mohammed — Prophet & founder of Islam

Saint Augustine — Ancient Christian theologian

Saint John — Apostle of Jesus & author

Saint Paul — Missionary & author of the early Christian church

Robert H. Schuller — Minister, founder of the Crystal Cathedral & inspirational author

John A. Shedd — Professor & author

W. Clement Stone — Businessman & motivational author

Blessed Teresa of Calcutta — Humanitarian & Nobel Laureate

Eckhart Tolle — Author & spiritual teacher

Oprah Winfrey — Television host & philanthropist

Working with the Formula
CEOx3R=PTSIT™

List ten **challenges** you are facing. If you can't list ten, list as many as you can.

1. ______________________________
2. ______________________________
3. ______________________________
4. ______________________________
5. ______________________________
6. ______________________________
7. ______________________________
8. ______________________________
9. ______________________________
10. ______________________________

Now select three challenges that you feel are insurmountable and keep you from moving forward.

Describe what you could do to **rise** to these challenges.

1. ______________________________
2. ______________________________
3. ______________________________

List one of your most memorable **experiences** you have ever had.

____

Describe how you felt while you were experiencing it. What made it outstanding?

____

List five **opportunities** that have recently come your way.

1. ______________________________________
2. ______________________________________
3. ______________________________________
4. ______________________________________
5. ______________________________________

What are some of the ways you could act on these opportunities?

____

____

What motivates you? List five practices which could motivate you into action.

1. ______________________________________
2. ______________________________________

3. ______________________________

4. ______________________________

5. ______________________________

How do you encourage others?

____

How do others encourage you?

____

What have you discovered about yourself?

____

How can you be enabled to take your next step?

____

What fulfills you?

____

Describe any "aha" moments you are having while working through this book.

____

____

www.ingramcontent.com/pod-product-compliance
Lightning Source LLC
Chambersburg PA
CBHW030827060726
47590CB00004B/1435

* 9 7 8 0 9 8 3 4 8 1 3 0 0 *